better together*

*This book is best read together, grownup and kid.

 akidsco.com

a
kids
book
about

a kids book about

death

by Taryn Schuelke

a
kids
book
about

Printed in the United States of America.

A Kids Book About books are available online: *akidsco.com*

To share your stories, ask questions, or inquire about bulk
purchases (schools, libraries, and nonprofits), please use
the following email address: *hello@akidsco.com*

ISBN: 978-1-951253-40-0

Designed by Duke Stebbins
Edited by Denise Morales Soto

Dedicated to our beloved, mine and yours,
who left our hearts forever changed.

Intro

Death can be one of the most difficult topics to discuss, no matter your age. It can feel especially intimidating to address it with kids. However, kids are ready to talk about it. They are able to understand death and cope with grief. I know this because I have dedicated my career and education to support families with this conversation.

This book helps explore what death is, how it makes us feel, and how we respond to it. I tried to keep it as simple as possible so that you and your kid can have deeper conversations about whatever topics matter most. You may want to pause for some of the questions so you may discuss further, or take a break. What kids need most when facing this topic is a trusted grownup who will be honest and sensitive.

Now, let's begin, together.

You just opened a kids book.

But it isn't a typical kids book.

This book is about...

death.

Just like every book has a beginning and an end, so does every living thing.

The end part is called death,

and sometimes it can be
really hard to talk about.

Why?

Because it can bring

BIG FEELINGS...

acceptance, heartbreak, sadness, confusion, envy, gloom, bother, certainty, aching, ease, powerlessness, eagerness, fulfilledness, caution, guilt, worry, awkwardness, sensitivity, sorrow, numbness, horror, devastation, interest, worry, bitterness, protectiveness, loss, humiliation, confidence, confusion, anger, crankiness, motivation, anxiety, astonishment, relief, challenge, jitters, hope, courage, gratification, strength, warmth, exhaustion, paranoia, impatience, nausea, shakiness, obsession, angst, playfulness, loneliness, hurt, reflection, fear, gratitude, embarrassment, shyness, neutrality, distress, love, grief, peace, snappiness, optimism, rage, agitation, intimacy, joy, compassion, pain, selfishness, anger, tension, defeat, hostility, fortune, hesitation, exclusion, regret, thankfulness, pride, fury, anticipation, curiosity, tiredness, neediness, distress, restlessness, helplessness, denial, calm...

Good feelings & hard feelings.

The truth is, there's no right or wrong way to feel about death.

In fact, people usually feel many feelings all at the same time.

Even grownups!

Actually, grownups can also have a hard time talking about death.

(Give your grownup a high five for being brave and getting you this book!)

I talk to people about death all the time.

I know that sounds weird, but it's my job!

I want to help you talk about death too,
and I hope this book will make that a little easier.

So, if you're ready, let's get started.

First, to understand death,
it's important to know what

alive

means.

To be alive means that
the body is working,
the mind is thinking,
and the person is feeling.

If you are reading this book,
that means you're alive!

Are you with me so far?
Great!

OK, now I'm going to describe what death means.

Imagine a flower
growing in a garden.

Its roots are connected to the
nutrients in the earth and its leaves
are absorbing the energy of the sun.

Then, the flower gets picked.

**What do you think will
happen to the flower?**

With time, the flower will die.

For people, it's kind of like that too.

Dying begins when important parts of the body stop working.

Like the lungs,
which breathe air.

Like the heart,
which pumps blood.

Like the kidneys and liver,
which clean the blood
(and other things).

Like the brain,
which tells the body what to do.

These are called vital organs.

Vital organs are super important!
When a vital organ stops working, it's called dying.

Other parts of the body can stop working and the person can be fine.

Like arms, eyes, ears, or toes.

Every living thing can get sick or hurt,
like when you catch a cold or break a bone.

That's normal!

Being sick or hurt is not the same as dying...

...Dying usually begins when one of these things happens:

People get really, really old,
and the body can't work anymore.

A big accident causes an
injury that stops the vital organs.

A person gets a serious illness
which is deadly to the body.

Or death can happen on purpose,
by suicide or violence.

Dying can happen quickly or it can happen slowly.

If death happens slowly, the dying person's body changes.

Their vital organs aren't working like they used to,
so the person might not be as hungry
or might be really tired all the time.

(That's OK!)

The dying body conserves energy, and we can help the person who is dying by creating a calm and comfortable environment.

So, how do we know if someone is dead?

Death happens when EVERYTHING stops working.

Dead means the body can't be alive anymore.

They can't eat, talk, feel, walk, or pick their nose...

All the things living people do.

No matter how someone dies, we honor and respect their body and take care of it after death.

There are many different ways
people take care of a dead body:

Some people have a funeral or memorial service
with songs, prayers, and thoughtful words.

A viewing of the body might happen.

It might be important to touch
or not touch the body.

Some people lay the body to rest right away,
others do so on a specific day after the death.

Some dead bodies are placed in tombs, others are buried in the ground.

It might be important to keep special items with the body.

Some people choose cremation for the body (which means turning the body into ashes).

And many other ways. It all depends on what the dying person wants or what their family chooses.

When it comes to death,
there is a lot to talk about.

Remember those BIG FEELINGS?

Have you felt any while thinking
about death or reading this book?

Now let me tell you the most important thing...

Death is normal.

When and how it happens can feel unfair,
but it's something that

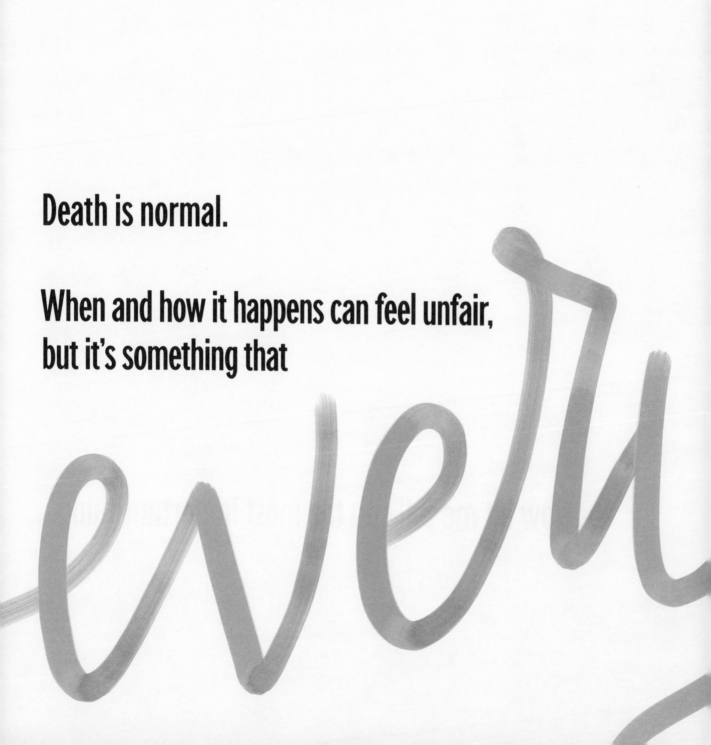
every

will experience. Death is a part of life.

Do you know someone who has died?

Do you know someone who is dying?

I want you to know that it's OK to talk about it.

Talking about dying or someone who has died can be really comforting and helpful.

You can remember
great moments
and special days.

You can celebrate
the person's life.

You can share stories,
wishes, and dreams.

When we talk about death
it creates community,
belonging, and family.

Talking about death
helps us think about what
we believe in. Like...

What is our purpose?

What is the meaning of life?

Is there something after death?

Is there a special part of us that continues on?

It helps us talk about what really matters.

One thing I know for sure is that death doesn't end a relationship.

I bet you're wondering,
how is that possible?!

Because love doesn't end with

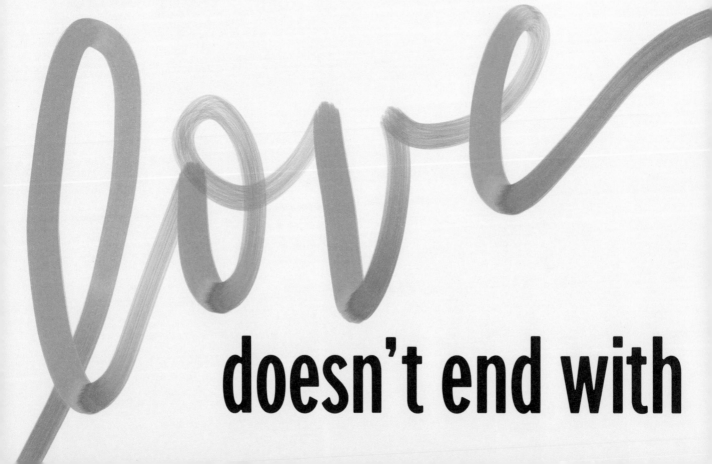

death. Love continues and grows and changes over time. Even after death.

This makes people feel and act in new ways.

(This is called grief.)

The things they decide to do, or say, or make out of that LOVE keeps the relationship going.

Why?

That LOVE only exists
because the relationship existed.

Life is like a story.

Just because the book closes
doesn't mean you forget what the
story was or the way it made you feel.

Death is normal
and it's OK to talk about it!

And if those BIG FEELINGS happen,
I hope you talk about those too.

Your thoughts matter.

Your feelings matter.

Your questions matter.

Your life matters.

IDEAS
TO KEEP THE LOVE GROWING AFTER DEATH:

Wear their favorite color.

Take a picture with their picture.

Visit their favorite place.

Write them a letter and keep it in a safe place.

Make a cake on their birthday.

Hold something that was theirs.

Think about them during important moments.

Tell stories about them.

Draw them a special picture.

Say their name to someone.

Eat their favorite food.

Listen to one of their favorite songs.

Outro

Brave grownup, if you are reading this book with an awesome kid, that means you are doing hard and meaningful things. Every loving caregiver I have worked with has struggled to start this conversation. That is the hardest part—starting.

Here is some advice I like to share with all of my fellow grownups who are talking about death with kids—keep it honest and keep it simple. Use their questions and thoughts as a guide. Explain details about the death, but only as much as you feel comfortable with. There is always time to explain further as your kid gets older. Starting with the basics and then adding more information as they are ready will help them not feel overwhelmed.

Keeping an open and honest space for talking about death will build trust with you and your kid and help them feel safe.

So I mean it when I call you brave. You are brave, and you can talk about difficult things. Thank you for helping kids feel safer, stronger, and smarter.